How-To-Start A Business: And Be Your Own Boss

DR. CARLETTA D. WASHINGTON

Copyright © 2014 Dr. Carletta D. Washington

All rights reserved.

ISBN: 1494732394
ISBN-13: 978-1494732394

DEDICATION

This book is dedicated to the Father, Son, and Holy Spirit. Starting and continuing Education 4 All, Inc. has been a spiritual journey. Through this process I have grown in ways which I strongly believe would not have been possible without the aid of the Holy Trinity!

This book is dedicated to my husband Freddie who has always supported Education 4 All, Inc. in every way possible, at each stage of its development. Thank you for believing in me and for helping me to carry out God's will. I love you!

This book is dedicated to my daughter Tierra who has always assisted with Education 4 All, Inc.—even as a child. Your involvement and input are greatly appreciated!

This book is dedicated to my mother Connie who has spent 3 years asking me when I was going to write my next book. Thank you for holding me accountable!

This book is dedicated to other family members: Aunt Maxine and Uncle Eddie II, Aunt Kaye and Uncle Stan, Bobie and his wife Michele, Eddie III, Kenny, Abigail, Nathan, Cheryl and in-laws Mary and Hubert who have supported Education 4 All, Inc. and kept it uplifted in prayer. Together, we have made a difference in the lives of many!

This book is dedicated to my friends and colleagues:
Dr. Shonta Smith (www.drshontasmith.com), Robert Jr., Douglas III, Niki, Esthere, Dr. Barnett, Lydia (www.booksbylydia.com), Ms. Henderson, and Dr. Rockel Etienne (www.rockeletienne.com) / (www.retrainingandconsulting.com) who have supported Education 4 All, Inc. and encouraged me in my journey. Your continued support keeps me motivated!

TABLE OF CONTENTS

DEDICATION
(PP. 4-5)

SPECIAL ACKNOWLEDGEMENT
(P. 9)

FOREWORD:
A LETTER TO CURRENT AND FUTURE
ENTERPRENEURS
(PP. 11-13)

CHAPTERS 1-11
(PP. 15-107)

BONUS TIPS
(PP. 109-112)

BUSINESS RESOURCES
(PP. 114-115)

AFTERWARD
(P. 117)

BUSINESS JOURNAL
(PP. 118-124)

ABOUT THE AUTHOR:
EDUCATION 4 ALL MOVEMENT
(PP. 126-133)

CHAPTER HEADINGS

Chapter 1
Determining Your Call, Part I..................................15

Determining Your Call, Part II.................................21

Chapter 2
Taking Care of the Basics.......................................26

Chapter 3
Investing in Your Business......................................36

Chapter 4
Finding Your Niche..41

Chapter 5
Selecting Quality People..51

Chapter 6
Being the CEO...56

Chapter 7
Attracting and Retaining a Paying Market..................73

Chapter 8
Systematizing Your Business...................................80

Chapter 9
Setting Your Priorities..88

Chapter 10
Making a Bold Move..94

Chapter 11
Planning for Your Business' Future..........................103

SPECIAL ACKNOWLEDGEMENT

This book is dedicated to my sisters in the National Sorority of Phi Delta Kappa, Inc. and the National Sorority of Phi Delta Kappa, Inc., Alpha Nu Chapter—St. Louis. Thank you for supporting Education 4 All!

This book is dedicated to my team of professionals Elaine Young of Hopscotch Communications (www.hopscotchcommunications.com) for logo design, Laurie for web design, and Odie Smith (www.mynubeginnings.com) for career coaching and IT assistance. Your commitment to quality service continues to increase the impact of the Education 4 All Movement!

FOREWARD

Dear Current and Future Entrepreneurs:

My experience as the CEO of my own non-profit education organization Education 4 All, Inc. is extremely rewarding! I learn a great deal, connect with wonderful people, and touch the lives of many through the Education 4 All movement! I am able to combine my passion for education and my interest in business into an amazing opportunity!

I am blessed to work with quality people along the way. They demonstrate pride in the work that they do for Education 4 All, Inc. and know me very well. In fact, whenever I am at a loss for ideas, these individuals prove to be more than capable when making a decision on my behalf. Their expertise never fails me!

Starting a business can be intimidating. When I first began Education 4 All, Inc., I found it somewhat difficult to understand the forms required for business registration. I also found limited access to information for small business entrepreneurs in the non-profit sector concerning how to actually set up and operate a business. Nevertheless, I am grateful that I have not given up, and that I have taken the opportunity to address the basics of my business, which is allowing me to focus on the development of my organization's services and products.

Perhaps, the most valuable lesson that I am learning as CEO of my own business is that marketing is paramount when it comes to a business' success. When I invest the right amount of money, time, and/or training into a project, the rewards are great! In terms of my business, this translates into having an increased number of attendees at an event, attendees leaving excited and ready to take action, and making a profit (or at least breaking even)! I am thrilled about the marketing systems that I am implementing as I work to continue to serve as a resource for my target market.

I recently made a bold move by leaving the workforce to pursue my business on a full-time basis. As a result of this decision, I am able to focus solely on my business, thinking and performing as the CEO of my own non-profit education organization Education 4 All, Inc. In addition, I am now able to implement a number of systems to ensure greater efficiency and effectiveness in my business. Most importantly, my priorities have shifted since working as the CEO of my own business on a full time basis; I neither neglect, nor over-commit myself. After 20 years, I now have a more balanced and more fulfilled life!

I look forward to what the future holds for Education 4 All, Inc. (www.education4allinc.com) and its movement to empower parents and educators to improve the academic success of students from pre-school through college. I truly believe that I am called to focus on improving student success, parental involvement, teacher retention, and community support. I pray that my movement and this book inspire you to pursue your own business!

Sincerely,

Dr. Carletta D. Washington
Personal & Professional Development Specialist

CHAPTER 1

DETERMINING YOUR CALLING, PART I

Many people make unwise business career decisions without ever really knowing what it is they are actually called to do. There are a few key reasons for this.

1. Chasing the money

Money should not be the number one motivator for starting a business. Money does not guarantee happiness. Some of our richest and most famous people prove this statement true on a rather frequent basis. Building a business requires time to grow and turn a profit. For many, the profit may be relatively small once expenses have been covered—particularly within the first few months (or early years) of one's company start-up date.

Sadly, some feel that the most lucrative business choice is where they should focus their energy and time; however, this might not be the career path best suited for them. That is why I often encourage young people to explore a variety of careers that are within their passion and interest. I ask them to focus more on their talents and gifts. Then, I encourage them to think of careers that utilize their unique talents and gifts. Finally, I ask them to select a career choice that they would pursue—even if they had to work in that field for FREE!

Of course, this is contrary to what many of us have been—and are currently—being taught. However, think about it: How many of us (or those whom we may know) have chosen high-powered, highly profitable career choices only to find little or no satisfaction thus, resulting in a mid-life career change? So, why not engage upcoming generations along a career development pathway that encourages them to chase their dreams and to turn their passion into their own business idea. *If you love what you do, you never work a day in your life.* If you market what you do well to your ideal market, the money will find you.

2. Fear

Many great inventors and business persons have failed repeatedly before being able to develop their most ingenious product or idea. Had they given up because of a fear of failure, fewer cars, computer programs, and other conveniences would exist today. In fact, some of these and others might not even exist at all today—if those behind their conception had given up on themselves, their idea, and/or their product.

The Bible tells us that "…God hath not given us the spirit of fear; but of power, and of love, and of a sound mind" (KJV). Therefore, if we truly believe that God has ordained our calling to do a particular work through a unique business endeavor, then why fear? Far too many of us have become used to a comfortable lifestyle as a result of trusting ourselves and others—instead of trusting God. Sometimes, being called to start a business is the way through which

God teaches us to trust Him. When God calls, rest assured, He will not only qualify us, but also provide for us. With God, there is nothing to fear!

3. Trying to be all things to all people

No one can do EVERYTHING. While many are aware of this, they never cease to try to achieve this ever-impossible task. Trying to do everything may give the impression that you are unfocused and incapable of providing the exact assistance that clients/customers need. Clients/Customers seek experts. In other words, they are seeking individuals who can meet their specific need by bringing resolve to their unique problem and/or concern.

Trying to accommodate everyone's needs also hinders your ability to fully develop in the area of greatest need for your potential clients/customers. While it appears to be a great and glorious feat to be able to address any issue at any time, it is far better to focus on 1 to 3 areas in which to gain expert knowledge and experience. In time, mastery in additional areas will naturally develop as you understand your target market and its growing needs.

4. Others' perspectives about our career path

Too often we allow others to determine our future. We may have our hearts set on becoming the next well-known inventor, landscape artist, or celebrity event planner, until we share our dreams with others and they *burst our bubble* by making statements such as: *you are not good enough; you won't make any money in that field; or you do not have the right training.*

Instead of sharing our dreams with our own limited group of family, friends, and associates, we need to share our dreams with those who are currently in our field of interest. Many are willing to share their insight and to serve as a mentor and/or offer apprenticeships, internships, and job-shadowing if we ask. Those who have been in the field for 3 years or more will be able to provide insight that is not normally found within a textbook or even within career exploration handbooks. So, if you really want to learn the *inside scoop* about any career, it is best to *go straight to the source!*

Sometimes, people project their own dreams or assumptions upon us regarding our future. For instance, moms may witness their daughter singing and dancing and automatically assume that she should focus on winning beauty pageants. A father who played high school or college football may notice how well his son plays football with his neighborhood friends and determine that his son should aspire to become a professional football player. While it is good to help foster our children's talents and gifts—as we perceive them to be—it is not a good idea to thrust any particular career choice upon our children. It is equally detrimental to expect our children to *walk in our footsteps*. Today's generation is not so eager to *carry on the family tradition* as it relates to their future career plans. Families must work together to develop a plan that will allow everyone to live their dreams.

Q & A

What's holding you back from pursuing/excelling in your career as the CEO of your own business venture?

DETERMINING YOUR CALLING, PART II

Let us examine a few ways in which we can prevent and/or resolve these issues so that we are better able to determine our calling with regard to our business endeavor as an entrepreneur and CEO.

1. Pray

It is best to seek God's guidance and direction in ALL that we do! When we read the Holy Bible, we see that everyone serving according to his/her calling was thoroughly equipped to serve in the capacity of their calling. Moses did not feel he could appropriately articulate the Lord's message to Pharaoh. However, because God had chosen Moses, He was able to counter each of Moses' arguments. This resulted in Moses being able to lead an entire nation of people out of slavery.

As you pray, you will discover that God has already blessed you with 1 or more spiritual gifts. These gifts are very special and are to be used for God's glory to benefit others. While many may have the same gift(s) as you, only you can use your gift(s) in the precise way in which God intended your gift(s) to be implemented. So, take time to pray and reflect on areas in which you are already operating in your gift(s) because that is the area in which you may be called to serve.

2. View your career path as a means of service to God and others

If we look at only what we hope to gain from our career choice, then we will *fall short* every time. Rewards come from service. As the Bible says, *we reap what we sow*. Our potential for internal, external, and eternal reward increases when we sow good seeds without expecting anything for ourselves in return. If we focus solely on the principle of *what's in it for me (WIFM)*, then we are living in selfishness. When God calls us, we must not ignore His calling or attempt to alter His plans. Much like in the case of Jonah, God's calling will prevail—despite our attitude and actions.

God not only speaks to man directly, but also indirectly through others. Therefore, it is best to survey our potential target market to determine its needs. This can help to fully open our eyes to what God has called us to do. Brief surveys and casual conversations with others whom you intend to serve will allow you to gain much needed information that can help you to focus your efforts on providing solutions to the problems and concerns of your potential clients/customers from their perspective. This is a winning formula for success!

3. Walk in your anointing

Even when you are not other people's first choice, if God has called you—you had better believe that He will *open doors for you* and *make a way out of no way*. That's what happened in the case of

King David. God had chosen David to eventually succeed King Saul's throne. Even though all of Jessie's most strong and valiant sons were presented to the Prophet Samuel, God prompted Samuel to ask Jessie if he had any other sons. Samuel sent for the young shepherd boy who was, perhaps, the least likely of Jessie's sons to be viewed as a king, in stature alone. Afterwards, David slew Goliath, won wars, and out-smarted King Saul prior to being awarded the throne. He had already demonstrated a potential for kingly success early on while tending sheep; however, his anointing helped to add to his credibility and boldness—regardless of what others may have felt about him initially.

Be confident in your anointing. Do not allow anyone to discredit you on the basis of your age, race, gender, etc. Be assured of your calling and walk boldly in your calling. *Be steadfast and unmovable.* God has promised to be with you—even in the midst of your enemies.

Q & A

What action can you implement so that you can begin to determine/excel in your calling TODAY?

_____
_____
_____
_____
_____
_____
_____
_____
_____
_____
_____
_____
_____
_____

CHAPTER 2

TAKING CARE OF THE BASICS

While it is true that you do not need business cards, a website, a marketing plan, or formal business training in order to enter into business, keep in mind that many of your potential clients/customers have adopted their perception of the ideal entrepreneur: the business person who is prepared as a result of proper planning, organization, training, and professional presentation. Clients/Customers who need assistance in resolving their problems and concerns are aware that they need to pay for services/products and often do not mind paying *top dollar* for *relief* from their burden—if the business has an authentic message, style, quality, and professional presentation.

Remember, as CEO, you are the face and brand for your company. How you present yourself will determine if a client/customer chooses to work with you and whether or not that same person agrees with paying you the monetary value you have associated with your services/products. It makes little sense to begin asking people to pay money for something that appears to be haphazardly put together. However, while it is not feasible for some entrepreneurs to be able to have everything they need for their business at the start, there are a few aspects of business that will make the difference and are worth your time, money, and training. As you continue through this chapter, notice how information from one step may be needed for the step that follows; business is logical and methodical in terms of organizing a company's basic structure. All that follows after the basics are in place depends on you—the CEO!

1. A suitable and catchy name

Throughout the Bible, names hold special meanings. So, should the name of your company. Your patrons should be able to easily associate your company's name with its mission, vision, and field of expertise. Your business' name should also be easy for your patrons to remember so that they think of your company before all others. Remember to complete the appropriate paperwork for registering your company's name to ensure that the name you have selected is available.

2. A suitable and appealing logo

What symbol best represents you and your company? Some ideas for a logo may include a house for a real estate agent or a freshly cut lawn decorated with a variety of flowers for a landscape artist. In some instances the first and/or last initial of the CEO's name or the company's title may best represent the company.

Whether your company's logo is commonly used in your field or is of abstract nature, tailor your logo to your company and make it as unique as possible in terms of color, size, text, etc. Your target market must be able to identify with your logo design without much effort. Remember to trademark your company's logo, particularly if it is an original design.

3. A Means of communicating with your patrons, lenders, and investors

Entrepreneurs who have decided to run a home-based business may not want to use their home address and phone number for privacy reasons. Honestly, an outside office location is not necessarily needed. However, it is wise to set up an e-mail account, rent a post office box, and order a separate business line in your home through your phone company, or extend the minutes on your cell phone plan. Doing so will provide a safe—yet professional—method for communicating with potential clients/customers, lenders (i.e., banks), and investors (i.e., philanthropists). If people are unable to communicate with you, they may be more inclined to purchase similar services and/or products from another business with which they can communicate.

4. An excellent Board of Directors

For many entrepreneurs, organizing the ideal Board consisting of key power players in the business and financial community may be a little difficult—unless you have a strong network and/or influence. Be aware that there are many types of Boards. However, new businesses often need a Board that functions more so as a *working Board*, which consists of a group of individuals who do not mind helping you to organize your business, plan and set-up events, fundraise, etc. These people may be with you in the beginning just to help your business to begin operation.

Over time, your Board may develop into more of a *governing Board*, consisting of members who are business executives, private donors, and community leaders who have expertise in legal matters, marketing, finance, human resources, and other areas, in which they provide limited assistance. Often these individuals' schedules only permit them to attend limited meetings either quarterly or annually. In addition, their other commitments may not permit them to be able to assist with the *day-to-day nuts and bolts* of your business' operations. However, regardless of your Board's funtion, be sure to select members who are as equally passionate and committed to your cause as you.

5. Incorporate, Incorporate, Incorporate

As CEO, you must determine how you will register your business. Although the paperwork and descriptions can be a little challenging, it is possible for you to complete this process without the aid of a lawyer. However, remember to read each description carefully to determine which type of corporation is most suitable so that you are able to best protect you, your family's assets, and your business. If you find later that you need to change your filing, you may always make any needed changes/updates. Also, complete your proposed budget, articles of incorporation, and by-laws for this process. If your business is a non-profit, be sure to complete paperwork for an advanced ruling with the IRS and sales tax exemption paperwork with your Secretary of State's office. All of the paperwork that you need is online and numbers for assistance are available.

6. A detailed business plan

Some entrepreneurs tend to skip this step or to only write a brief proposal. Your business plan is your company's *meal ticket*. The more detailed the plan, the more likely lenders and investors are to support your company's efforts. Writing a detailed business plan demonstrates seriousness on your part and dispels any doubts and/or misconceptions on the part of potential lenders, investors, and patrons. It is possible for you to write your own business plan based upon various models and examples on the Internet; however, be sure that your plan is specific to your business. Also, seek professional assistance as needed to help ensure a quality plan that lenders and investors will be more apt to accept.

7. A user-friendly website

A website is advisable. Potential clients/customers, lenders, and investors want to feel as though they can connect with you and learn about your company without having to first contact you directly. Therefore, you must have a user-friendly website! Visitors who experience difficulty navigating through your site, may choose not to support your company. Keep the number of pages to a minimum. Embellish your website with colors that are common to your field, technological trends such as slide show banners that accurately illustrate your company's mission and vision, and buttons for a newsletter subscription, visitor tracker, Facebook, LinkedIn, Amazon, PayPal, etc. Use consistent font for headings, subheadings, and details. If incorporating music, be sure to respect copyright laws and to select music that is appropriate for your particular site and type of business. Also, update your website as needed. Reviewing your competitors' sites can serve as inspiration so that your business' site remains current.

8. Business cards

A business card is an excellent marketing tool that should be with you at all times in case you meet a potential lender, investor, or client/customer. Be sure to use the space on your business card wisely and leave some empty space—the entire card does not need to be filled with words and images. Also remember to use quality paper and printing; a double-sided, high-gloss, full-color, heavy-weight paper/card stock is recommended. People tend to expect more and are willing to pay more for services/products simply based on the quality of a person's business cards.

9. Bank account

A business account will help to accurately track monthly assets and liabilities. It will also add legitimacy to your business in that there will be a checking account, a debit card, and possibly a credit card with a line of credit in your business' name. A business account will also allow for separation of your personal and business finances.

10. On-line merchant account

An on-line merchant account such as PayPal will permit you to invoice your patrons so that they may purchase goods and services directly from your company. Best of all, since your on-line merchant account is connected to your business' bank account, funds can be automatically deposited into your account. Your merchant account can also be linked to your website to help generate sales directly from your site. Investors can also make donations to your business through your on-line merchant account. Additionally, merchant accounts work with mobile transaction devices (i.e., Square), making it easy for *on-the-spot* transactions.

11. Insurance

Whether you are working from your home or an outside office, business insurance is extremely important! Speak to a reputable insurance agent to determine the right type and amount of coverage for you and your business needs. Liability insurance is also equally important for protecting yourself and your business from legal action. If you hire employees, workers' compensation will be another type of insurance to consider. Depending on your situation, you may need to explore health/medical and life insurance plans. Protection is paramount!

12. Business code information

Familiarize yourself with your subdivision, city/municipality, state/providence, and country's business codes. This will help you to avoid potential delays, closure, and/or added expenses. For instance, some residential neighborhoods will not grant business licenses for in-home daycares and other businesses because of existing residential and commercial zoning laws. There are also fire codes pertaining to the maximum number of people who can be serviced at any given time, and codes for wheel chair accessibility, etc. Knowing and abiding by these codes is important for your business' success and longevity.

Q & A

Use the chart below to indicate the completion date for each item pertaining to your business. If an item has not been completed, write in your target date for completion.

Item	Date Completed/ Target Date for Completion
Suitable & catchy name	
Suitable & appealing logo	
Means of communication	
Board of Directors	
Incorporation/Business Registration	
Business plan	
User-friendly web site	
Business cards	
Bank account	
On-line merchant account	
Insurance	
Codes for business operation	

CHAPTER 3

INVESTING IN YOUR BUSINESS

1. Time

Building a business—especially one that sustains itself—takes time. Unfortunately, some entrepreneurs expect to build a stable lucrative business within a matter of weeks or months. You must be patient. Although the length of time to reap a profit varies by business (and other factors), as long as your business has the proper foundational structure and systems in place, it should not take very long to experience success.

Spend your time wisely. There are only 24 hours in any given day for every individual living on the planet. Determine the number of hours that are needed in order to build and operate your business. Unfortunately, many entrepreneurs find themselves working every aspect of their business. While no one really intends to work his/her business by him/herself, this is the reality during much of the start-up phase. As time progresses, the number of hours needed to complete certain tasks will shift once your systems are in place and you have at least 1 assistant/employee (other than yourself). Therefore, until you can afford a marketing expert, grant writer, office assistant, and/or program director, it is wise that you allocate a great deal of time in these areas to help generate business which results in a profit so that you will be able to hire quality individuals who can assume these responsibilities and others in the future.

2. Money

Money is extremely pertinent to the success of any business. No matter your budget, your money must be spent wisely. Your funds must only be spent on things that will bring true benefit to your business and allow it to move forward. Know that paying a lot for a particular service or product does not necessarily guarantee quality. On the other end of the spectrum, something that is relatively inexpensive may be of high quality.

Also, remember to invest money into all aspects of your business (marketing, in particular) so that all areas are addressed. Most importantly, set your budget for each area, and stay on budget as much as possible. It is important to make accurate estimations (or near-accurate guestimates). Finances in terms of budgeting and a keen sense of financial projections are vital in maintaining your business.

3. Training

Be sure to get the appropriate education and/or training required for your company's success. Pursing a degree, attending continuing education courses at a community college, listening to on-line business coaches, seeking a mentor, shadowing an expert, borrowing books from the library or purchasing them from bookstores, surfing the Net, attending conferences, and asking questions can really benefit you as CEO. Training can vary in terms of money needed for registration and time needed for completion. Therefore, you must find what will work best for your schedule, without taking an extensive amount of time and money away from your business. Too much training can become extremely time-consuming and expensive. Your business will not be on the road to success until you actually begin to implement what you learn from your training. Remember that while investing money into additional training may be necessary, you may also need to simultaneously invest money into other areas of your business, so choose your training programs wisely.

Q & A

Step 1:
Complete the pie chart based upon the current percentage of <u>time</u>, <u>money</u>, and <u>training</u> that you have invested into your business. *Be sure the entire chart adds up to 100%.

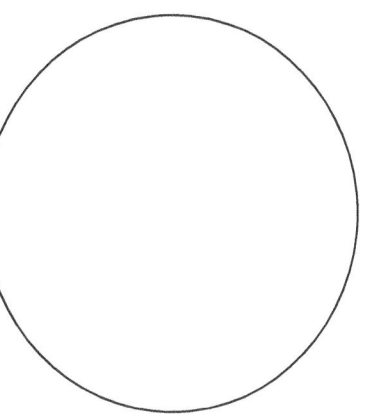

Step 2:
If your business <u>is</u> successful, which area(s) has/have contributed to the success of your business: time, money, and/or training?

_____
_____
_____

If your business is <u>not</u> as successful as you would like, to which area(s) do you feel you should direct more attention: time, money, and/or training?

_____
_____
_____

CHAPTER 4

FINDING YOUR IDEAL NICHE

No one can appeal to everyone. Even in stores that cater to teens, there is a variety of styles because the marketing experts for those particular stores know that one style of clothing (and even one size) *does not fit all.* While diversification is good, the store in the aforementioned example is still only targeting one segment of the population: teens. As in the example, you, too, will need to decide your niche and determine the variety of offerings your niche prefers.

Sometimes, it seems as if there are too many of the same type of business in a particular area or field. Take a drive through a commercial area and note the number of beauty salons, mini malls, gas stations, or fast food restaurants located within a few feet of each other. Also, notice how there is more than enough patrons for each. Well, the same is true for you whether you want to be a consultant, web designer, author, virtual assistant, or retailer. There are more than enough clients/customers for you and the many other businesses similar to yours. All you have to do is find your ideal niche and cater to those specific clients/customers and their needs.

1. Who?

Who do you prefer to work with? This is an extremely important question! If you speak to any teacher, doctor, dentist, nurse, or barber, they will have an immediate answer: babies, toddlers, children, teens, adults. They will also readily provide unsolicited justification for why they enjoy one particular group more so than the others. These individuals have learned that in order to be successful in their field, they must enjoy working with the group that they have selected.

Selecting a specific target market will permit you to refine your marketing strategy and to focus your efforts in a specific area, so that you avoid becoming overwhelmed and/or burned out in your own business. The time it takes to work in one specific area versus the time required to work in several areas is far less. As the saying goes, *work smarter, not harder*.

2. What?

What problem or issue does your ideal market want resolved? What can you do to help them through the process? These questions are the basis for your business' very existence. If there is no problem to be solved, then there is no need for any business solution. For instance, the invention of today's more modern versions of the original mop allows busy families to save time and energy completing the daily/weekly household chore of mopping. Other products serve more than one purpose. For instance, teens, adults, beauty professionals, health experts, scientists, artists, and media outlets use make up for a number of preventative and corrective enhancement purposes in an array of instances.

Viewing your business as the answer to someone's problem will enable you to remain focused on the needs of your patrons. Remember to place their needs first. After all, their loyalty and support will help to sustain your business. So think carefully about the types of services and/or products you will need to provide, and then be sure this is what you can and are willing to actually deliver.

3. Where?

Where do your potential clients/customers, lenders, and investors meet, reside, work, shop, play, exercise, etc.? Wherever they are—you need to be (However, do not compromise your moral integrity.). Networking is an on-going activity. Each day, we are surrounded by scores of people. This is our opportunity to introduce ourselves to at least 5 new people each day. Our chance encounters can translate into sales and profits, if we are *in the right place at the right time*!

Another fact to consider is where your clients/customers are willing to meet in order to receive your services and/or products. For instance, if you are a massage therapist, do your clients prefer to meet at your home or in an actual office building (Know that in this instance, your gender may influence their decision.)? Make sure the location of your business is safe and well-lit, especially if you are seeking to work with children, women, and/or the elderly. Be sure there is ample parking, and that it is accessible from major roads and highways. Furthermore, be sure that the physical space will allow you to properly accommodate your clients/customers, staff, program, technology, and equipment needs.

4. When?

Timing is everything. You can visit all of the right places, but if you are not frequenting the places where your potential patrons, lenders, and investors can be found at the time when most of them are present, you are wasting your time. For instance, if you want to market to young professions who work out at the local gym, you may want to work out at the gym either before or at the end of the work day. You might not find very many in your niche available during mid-day. On the other hand, if your ideal market is stay-at-home moms who have school-age children, then they might be found in record numbers at the gym during mid-day sessions.

Think about your ideal market's habits and schedules so that you can be available to them at a time that best suits their needs. If your market is only available after 5pm, it is futile to offer training sessions at 3pm. By surveying your ideal market and reviewing your schedule, you should be able to select a time that works best for both of you—with little compromise on your part.

5. Why?

Always be prepared to share why potential clients/customers should choose your service/product or why potential lenders and investors should financially support your company. If you cannot clearly articulate your company's value and worth, you may lose sales. Also, be confident in your response. Do not stumble or pause when explaining why you are the solution to others' problems. This is an excellent opportunity to gain others' attention and trust. If you appear not to believe your own message, then why should others?

Why do you want to assist your particular market of interest? What about this particular group draws you to them? Does this have anything to do with your past experiences or interests? Do not be afraid to share with your patrons, lenders, and investors why you are interested in working with them. Be genuine and upfront; transparency builds trust.

6. How?

How do you intend to reach your niche once you have its attention? Social media, e-blasts, e-zines, virtual events, live events, community bulletin boards, flyers, radio, and direct mail are some of the many potential ways to generate business. However, consider using the modes of communication that your ideal niche is most apt to use.

Determine how much support and how often your clients/customers will need the support of your services and/or products. Will your professional relationship be on a one-time basis, as-needed basis, or on-going basis? This may require you to adjust your hours and/or the duration of your programs and promotions so that you are able to best meet your niche's needs.

Q & A

1. Who is your ideal market?

_____
_____
_____
_____
_____

2. What problem or concern does your ideal market need and/or want resolved?

_____
_____
_____
_____

3. What is your solution to your ideal market's problem or concern?

_____
_____
_____
_____
_____
_____
_____

4. List all of the places where you will most likely be able to find your ideal market.

_____
_____
_____
_____
_____

5. Where will you most likely need to offer your products and/or services once you reach your ideal market?

_____
_____
_____
_____
_____

6. When is your market most likely available?

_____
_____
_____
_____
_____

7. When would you prefer to offer your products and/or services?

_____
_____
_____
_____

8. Why should your ideal market choose you versus your competitors?

_____
_____
_____
_____
_____
_____

9. Why do you want to help the market that you have chosen to target?

_____
_____
_____
_____
_____
_____

10. How do you plan to communicate with your ideal market?

_____
_____
_____
_____
_____
_____
_____
_____

11. How much support are you willing and able to provide to your ideal market and how often?

_____
_____
_____
_____
_____
_____
_____
_____
_____

CHAPTER 5

SELECTING QUALITY PEOPLE WHO...

1. Provide quality at every stage

While it is true that *you get what you pay for,* it is highly recommended that if budget is a concern, you find people who provide high quality work—regardless of an individual's budget. While service providers may offer different packages and levels of service for each pay increment—the level of quality should never fluctuate. For instance, a web designer should present a high quality website to fit into ANY budget! Whether a client pays him/her $30/h or $5,000 for the entire project, the resolution of the images and background should be of exceptional quality. What may vary at each degree of payment are the number of pages, links, edits, embellishments (i.e., font colors, slide shows, background music), hosting options, etc.—but never quality!

2. Have expertise

Some entrepreneurs on low budgets make the mistake of selecting individuals with virtually no experience. As entrepreneurs, we cannot trust our business to family members, friends, associates, and other people's friends simply because they offer their services at an inexpensive rate. Even though recommendations are wonderful, be sure to view the person's portfolio, work samples, and credentials yourself. If you do not sense the level of quality you are seeking, consider another provider IMMEDIATELY! Do not compromise—not for friends or budget.

3. Support their patrons

First of all, be honest with yourself about your budget. Do not contact a marketing or legal firm whose client base consists of celebrities, top-level executives, and Fortune 500 companies. It is unrealistic to expect that these service providers (retailers included) will support clients with low budgets. Therefore, search for businesses that will work with your particular budget, and be truthful about your budget so that there is no room for misunderstanding. In addition to a phone conference and/or face-to-face visit, be sure to communicate through e-mail and/or a written contract for clarity.

Also, be sure to select individuals who believe in your company and the project with which you would like assistance. The businesses and individuals whom you seek to work with should take a personal interest in your project. If they do not feel genuinely connected to your project, its quality may be compromised. Service providers who support their clients will also work to make sure their clients are happy throughout the entire process.

4. Are trustworthy

A lack of trust does not depend solely on justifiable violations of policy and/or morals; it can also result from two people not seeing *eye-to-eye* or one party not wanting to relinquish control of a project to another. If during the initial consultation or any stage of business, you feel uncomfortable or concerned about a company you have chosen work with, then ask questions, request a refund (partial or full), or walk away and cut your losses. Do not remain in any professional relationship where there is a lack of trust on either party's side. Even if you are providing a service or product for someone, and you feel that he/she does not trust your judgment and insight, then end the relationship as professionally as possible in order to avoid undue stress and other potentially unforeseen problems.

Q & A

Step 1:

What type of assistance do you need for your business?

_____
_____
_____
_____
_____
_____
_____
_____

Step 2:

List individuals whom you know that may be able to assist you based on the following:

- **quality performance, expertise, supportiveness, and trustworthiness.**

_____
_____
_____
_____
_____
_____
_____

CHAPTER 6

BEING THE CEO

Whether you decide to enter into business on a full-time basis or transition into your business over a period of time while hanging onto your *day job*, you must remember that you are the CEO of your business!

1. Be yourself

If you are not being yourself, then others will notice. They may not tell you personally. Instead, what they may do is avoid doing business with you or lose interest in working with you and end their professional relationship with you. Remember that you are the face of your company, so how you present yourself to others is crucial. If people do not perceive you to be approachable, professional, knowledgeable, trustworthy, honest, qualified, genuine, and so on, then your business may not prosper as much as you anticipated.

2. Stay true to your mission and vision

Avoid refining your original message so much so that neither you, nor anyone else can identify with you as CEO. When you determine your calling, it should truly reflect who you are as a person. Business is about making profits through lasting professional relationships with the aid of personal branding. If you are inconsistent in your presentation and message, you can confuse your existing clients/customers. In fact, some of your patrons will leave because they may feel that they are no longer able to connect with you since they do not know who you are anymore.

It is okay to critique and refine your branding, however. This is something that should be done on a frequent basis. If you find that you need to make changes, then by all means, please do. The key is that the overall message should not significantly *morph* into something completely different and unrecognizable to your existing client/customer base. You do not want to lose them.

3. Value yourself, your time, and your services and/or products

Do not allow others to monopolize your time and underestimate your worth. You started your business so that you could work on your own terms and on your own time schedule while making money in the process. Though spending hours listening to others' problems and giving them free advice seemed natural before you formed your business, it is not advisable now that you are the CEO of an official business. The days of FREE advice on a whim must become limited!

Doctors, lawyers, and thousands of other professionals bill for their time: doctors $25 co-pay, lawyers a $500 retainer. Granted these fees may go towards the actual cost of services, but they are paid upfront and are nonrefundable. No matter how close or how long the professional relationship between a person and his/her doctor or lawyer, he/she is still required to pay these upfront fees because of overhead (i.e., utilities, rent, equipment and supplies, salaries and benefits).

Likewise, do not hesitate to state your nonrefundable consultation fee at the start of any conversation that goes beyond 15 or 30 minutes because a lengthy conversation will require additional time away from your business. Politely invite your potential client/customer to a special one-to-one consultation session to determine his/her specific needs and your ability to address those needs in a more formal setting, and inform him/her of the session rate (i.e., $100 or $250 an hour), and that this time will be solely dedicated to his/her needs. Also, inform the client/customer that he/she must pay all or part of the non-refundable fee prior to the visit, at the start of the visit, or at the end of the session on the day of the visit.

If the individual is unable to pay, then offer a payment schedule or politely thank him/her for calling you and add that you will be available should his/her situation change. The bottom line is that you do not want to underestimate your worth and the value of your services/products by continuing to *give away* what you intend to SELL! While providing free sessions can be helpful in attracting clients/customers, be sure to convert these sessions into profit as a way of valuing yourself, your time, and your services/products and expanding your business.

Also, do not feel obligated to suggest a less-expensive service or retail provider within your industry. If you receive an affiliate fee, then by all means—refer away when needed so that you get at least a little something as a result of the encounter. However, do your best to focus solely on your business and its needs before venturing into the affiliate market. You do not want to be known as a referral company, unless that is your company's mission.

4. Plan your day, week, month, and year

This is not as difficult as you may think. The most important tool you need is a calendar—not just on your phone, but an actual physical 12-month calendar so that you can write down concrete business activities and plan what you expect to accomplish within each day, week, month, and year. As CEO, you always want to be able to see the *big picture*. The other important tool you need is a pencil. Be sure to use a pencil when writing your activities so that your calendar is both flexible and neat at all times. Using a pencil will allow you to erase activities and reschedule them in case of emergencies. The third tool is post-it notes, a note pad, or a notebook so that you can record daily tasks.

Remember to commit time each day to your business. Nothing will get done—if you do not do it yourself. Set aside dedicated hours for your business and be as consistent as possible in working those hours each day. The joy of being CEO is that you determine your own schedule and *you answer to no one other than yourself*! When you feel you have done enough for the day—even if it took less time than you intended, know that it is okay to postpone the next project or to *close up shop* early if you have completed everything on your agenda for the day.

While you are scheduling your business activities, be sure to schedule time off. You know ... personal days and vacations. Every CEO needs a break in order to refresh him/herself. Personal days and vacations help to inspire new ideas for business. It may even afford you the opportunity to meet new business contacts and/or partners in other cities, states, and countries.

5. Use your existing connections

Do not hesitate to connect with your family, friends, Church members, past and present co-workers, fraternity/sorority/league members, golf/basketball buddies, grocery store manager, retail owner, high school/college alumni, postal worker, social media friends, and any other person with whom you have had frequent contact in recent years. Do not look for their approval or suggestions! Simply introduce your idea with confidence as if *your life depends on it*. Actually, your life does depend on it from a financial and business perspective. So, view everyone in your many circles of association as potential clients/customers, lenders, and/or investors.

Do not shy away from using your circle of influence as a business connection. Remember the times when your nieces, nephews, grandchildren, or co-workers asked you to *buy another box of cookies or wrapping paper*? Same concept! If those around you trust this tried and true model, then why not you—it does work—you ordered last year, didn't you?

6. Find a dedicated office space

Even if you are working from home, every CEO is entitled to his/her own private office space! Work in a spare bedroom, dining room, attic space, closet, shed, or garage until you can afford an actual separate physical location. For those who do not have the extra space at home, use your kitchen table or a folding table as dedicated office space. If that does not work, take your office on the road. Work at your local library where you will have access to free Wi-Fi, computers, copiers, reference materials, and restrooms. Or, work at your local coffee shop, restaurant, or mall food court. These places offer free Wi-Fi, restrooms, and sometimes a few other business services. However, keep in mind that you may be asked to purchase something to eat or drink.

If you have the money to pay for dedicated office space, consider sharing a space or subletting space from another business to save on expenses. If you prefer your own space, then lease only what you need to start with, you can look for a larger office once your profits have increased. The advantages of moving to another location is that you will have established yourself in one community of loyal patrons and their patronage will help to pay expenses for your new larger office until you are able to secure new clients/customers.

Whether your space is temporary or permanent, at home or in a separate building, do not underestimate the value of having your own office space. There is nothing like arranging your work environment to suit your personal business needs as CEO of your own company! When you operate in your own space, you are able to fully transition into your role as CEO of your company.

7. Develop a CEO mindset

How you think about your business will impact your business. Therefore, it is vital that you begin to think like an actual CEO. Before you make any decision about your business, ask yourself: What would a successful CEO do? How would he/she respond? Next, think about the type of business and environment that you want to create. Once you develop a CEO mindset, you will begin to experience success. Regardless of how many hats you wear in the start-up phase of your business—you are still the CEO. So, do not be afraid to think and act as such. Embrace your title and the mindset of the type of CEO that you aspire to be!

8. Network with other CEOs

Developing relationships with other CEOs both inside and outside of your industry can be of benefit to you and the growth of your business. This is how some restaurateurs get the best deals on their products, which allows them to increase their profit margin; several have a solid working relationship with local fishermen and local farmers' markets. Some even engage in a bit of bartering. For instance, a restaurateur may invite his suppliers to a dinner prepared especially for them. In return, they may offer him first pick of their goods at the start of the season, perhaps at a discounted rate.

Think about what you have to offer to others in exchange for goods or services that you may need. For instance, if your business is a nonprofit, emphasize to potential donors the value of a tax letter—particularly at the end of the calendar year when many are seeking a tax write-off. There are many creative ways to barter until you have the funds to purchase what your business needs. Bartering can continue with your trusted partners even after you begin to see substantial profit, just be careful not to take advantage of the individuals and their kindness and that the relationship is mutually beneficial.

9. Choose your team wisely

This first team is most important! Every high-powered CEO has an excellent legal, financial, marketing, and consulting team. Just as these individuals and their firms prevent sparks from becoming fires, they also *put out fires*. Mistakes are bound to happen. While you may not have enough money to retain such a team, you will need to *shop around* until you find affordable quality individuals in the professional areas for which you need assistance. Do NOT underestimate the value of adding these individuals to your team of experts.

If you thoroughly prepare yourself and your business—and take your time, then you may not need to utilize the services of this professional team on a regular basis. For instance, you may only need your lawyer to review a few of your start-up documents. You may only need a CPA to do your taxes on an annual basis. You may only need a marketing guru to help establish your brand in the start-up stage of your business. You may only need a business consultant or coach to help you understand how to attract clients/customers at the onset of your business. Know that every relationship in the business world is not necessarily meant to be permanent.

The next team you need to build is a team of volunteers and/or unpaid interns if you cannot afford to hire anyone. Be sure to implement a quality volunteer and/or intern screening and hiring system so that you can attract quality candidates. Also, only build the team based on your needs. Being realistic about your business' needs will ensure greater success.

10. Know your competition

When you know your competition, you gain a wealth of knowledge about your ideal market. Learn everything you can about your competition. Review their websites, facilities, social media, stats, etc. so that you can evaluate your own business. Does your website need to be updated? What impression do first-time clients/customers get when they enter into your place of business? Are you connecting with your social media followers effectively? What do your numbers look like? Use the information that you obtain during the process of getting to know your competition to help improve your business and how it functions. Your competitors and even your potential clients/customers, lenders, and investors are evaluating all of those competing for their products, services, attention, time, and money, so do not be *left in the dark*.

Q & A

1. Describe your personality.

_____
_____
_____
_____
_____
_____

2. What is your business' mission?

_____
_____
_____
_____
_____
_____
_____
_____
_____
_____

3. What is your business' vision?

_____
_____
_____
_____
_____
_____
_____
_____
_____
_____

4. What dollar amount do you feel accurately describes your value and the value of your time, services, and/or products?

_____
_____
_____
_____

5. List business-related tasks that you intend to complete today, this week, this month, and this year.

_____

_____

_____

_____

_____

_____

_____

_____

_____

_____

_____

_____

_____

_____

6. List people/businesses you know personally that may be in need of your services and/or products.

_____
_____
_____
_____
_____
_____
_____
_____
_____
_____
_____
_____
_____
_____

7. Where will your place of business be located?

_____
_____
_____
_____

8. Describe 3 major decisions concerning your business do you need to make right now as the CEO?

_____
_____
_____
_____
_____
_____
_____
_____
_____
_____
_____
_____

9. List 3 CEOs (from any type of business) you will connect with over the next 5 days.

_____
_____
_____
_____

10. What team of experts do you need to build at this stage of your business?

_____
_____
_____
_____
_____
_____
_____
_____

11. List 3 businesses in your area that may be competing for your ideal market's attention.

_____
_____
_____
_____
_____
_____
_____
_____

CHAPTER 7

ATTRACTING AND RETAINING A PAYING MARKET

No matter your business, you need clients/customers. Without them, there is no profit. Much of the way you attract clients/customers is in the relationship you build with them through your branding, products, and/or services. How you market and promote your business is vital to your company's profitability and sustainability.

1. Use your prospective clients'/customers' language

Many remember actor Chris Tucker's famous line in *Rush Hour*, 'Do you understand the words that are coming out of my mouth?' With regard to entrepreneurs and their market, if your prospective clients/customers do not understand what you are saying, then they may choose not to do business with you. So, eliminate jargon that is used amongst the professionals within your field. Instead, use everyday language and descriptors that your potential market uses on a regular basis. It is possible to maintain a professional image while borrowing a few of the terms and phrases that your market uses (i.e., cool, super cute, hot, bling). People are more apt to buy from you if they feel you and your business genuinely appreciates them and understands their needs.

2. Listen to your market

You can listen to your market by conducting brief surveys so that you can gather all of the important information that you are seeking. Do not be afraid to use on-line survey tools through Google, Survey Monkey, etc. You may also consider organizing focus groups so that you can pitch an upcoming idea and receive your market's input.

Another way to listen to your market is by analyzing its buying trends. If you notice a product or service is out-selling another product or service, either revamp the one that is not doing as well or consider eliminating it from your offerings. Also, compare purchasing data across age, gender, income, profession, holidays, months, seasons, time of day, and even by year so that you can make a well-informed decision about the continuation and/or discontinuation—and even introduction—of a product or service. For example, you may find that while teen girls are the number one buyers of ballet flats, they are most willing to purchase them only during homecoming, prom, and the summer months. This data is extremely valuable for your inventory and sales departments.

The retention rate of your purchasing market says a great deal about your business. If your market is *leaving in droves*, then there is a problem! Find out what you are missing or are no longer providing (i.e., prompt service, personal guarantees, discounts, new trends), and change your strategy immediately! Returning clients/customers potentially lead to new clients/customers because repeat supporters spread the word to new prospects. Besides, who better to sell your products and/or services than those who are already purchasing and using them?

3. Address your clients'/customers' needs

Your clients/customers are coming to you because they want you to help them to resolve a problem, address an issue, or meet an unmet need. Building your business around helping people to resolve their problems, address their issues, and meet their unmet needs is a formula for success; it is a win-win situation! Once you focus your business around this model, prospective clients/customers will begin to see the value in what you have to offer—and their money will follow.

Be ready to offer a variety of programs and/or services that can assist you in serving your clients/customers both now and in the future. Your patrons' needs will determine the types of programs and/or length of services you offer. Remember, the goal is to be client/customer-centered. Once you have established a relationship with them, they will continue to patronize your business. So offer a mix of freebies, low-cost, and higher-cost products and/or services both online and in person in order to encourage your clients/customers to remain loyal patrons. This will produce a steady stream of income for you and your business.

4. Share your experiences

Feel free to share with your market how and why you entered into business. Include details and embrace your past as part of your decision to start your business. You never know how you may inspire your market to both act and even pursue its own business endeavors, which could benefit you *down the road*. Be humble and genuine in relating your story. Discuss what you have learned and how you have used that knowledge in your business. When you open up to your prospective clients/customers, they will become more open to working with you.

5. Be persistent

Continue to look for new clients/customers on a daily or weekly basis. Include promotions on a periodic basis to your potential clients/customers. Include extended offers or guarantees. Include free gifts. Use social media, phone calls, e-mails, thank you notes, and V.I.P./appreciation days to follow-up with existing and potential clients/customers. This will communicate your continued interest in them. When it appears that all the giving is only on your end, it may be time for you to move on to other prospective clients/customers. However, do not give up or become discouraged. Persist in finding new clients/customers so that you may continuously build your business.

Q & A

Step 1:

List 2 activities, programs, products, and/or services that you plan to implement in the upcoming days or weeks in order to <u>attract</u> a paying market.

_____
_____
_____
_____
_____
_____
_____
_____
_____
_____
_____
_____
_____
_____
_____
_____
_____

Step 2:

List 2 activities, programs, products, and/or services that you plan to implement in the upcoming weeks or months in order to <u>maintain</u> your paying customer/client base.

_____
_____
_____
_____
_____
_____
_____
_____
_____
_____
_____
_____
_____
_____
_____
_____
_____

CHAPTER 8

SYSTEMATIZING YOUR BUSINESS

Every entrepreneur must have a set of systems in place to ensure that his/her business runs as efficiently and effectively as possible. Your business must be able to function even without you being physically present in the office each and every day. It is best to have systems in place at the onset of your business so that you do not find yourself delaying important tasks in order to address a crisis or need that may arise. Failure to systematize your business can translate into a loss of revenue, potentially resulting in the inability to pay yourself, your staff, and other business-related financial obligations.

1. Job Descriptions

Be clear on your job description and how you will function at each stage of your business as its CEO. *Begin with the end in mind*, the point of success where you actually want to be and then work your way backwards to where you are at the current moment. We often view our future role of CEO in terms of a position of influence and even leisure. In the latter stages, your time should be dedicated to only a few major tasks such as overseeing department leaders and operations. If this is your vision, decide what business operations you actually want to address and oversee personally in the latter stages of your CEO career.

Next, look at where you are now. Determine the duties that you absolutely need to do in order to get your business started and to keep it *running smoothly*. The difference between the duties you anticipate in the distant future and those that you have in the beginning is great. During the start-up phase of your business, you may be required to assume several small, entry-level tasks in addition to the major responsibilities associated with operating a successful business.

Now that you have defined your start-up and future duties as your company's CEO, it is time to determine your role at mid-career. You will need to transition from overloading yourself in the beginning into obtaining the enviable leisurely role near the end of your career. Part of transitioning is to learn to delegate and to specialize in what you truly enjoy and desire to do within your company as its CEO. As you determine this potential job description, you should see no evidence of the time-consuming entry-level tasks that you need to fulfill in the beginning of your career as CEO of your company. At the midpoint of your CEO career, you should also be able to delegate some of the major duties, depending on your budget, staff, and interests. This *drilling down* of responsibilities will allow you to successfully transition into an easier and more leisurely CEO role in your company during your latter years.

Job descriptions will be needed for other staff members—regardless of their function within your company. Part of determining the job description will include first deciding the type of help that you will need as your company experiences growth (i.e., secretarial, public relations, technology). Then, consider your budget. Some titles appear to be more prestigious than others and infer a higher education level, thus requiring greater compensation for anticipated duties. Therefore, the job description you select will need to accurately reflect the budget that you will have available in order to meet payroll. For instance, you will need someone to answer the phone, check e-mails, schedule appointments, greet clients, accept applications, etc. So, do you assign that person the title of Administrative Assistant, Secretary, Executive Secretary, Office Coordinator, or Office Manager? There have been many different connotations attached to each of these titles throughout workforce history. In fact, a few may have come to your mind as you read each title.

Do not feel that you have to adjust the duties for one title over the other. If you later expand and are able to hire more than one employee for each department and/or position, then you can vary the titles, duties, and pay schedule. Until then, everyone who is hired in the early stages will need to accept that they are responsible for all of the duties that you have assigned at the rate that you are able to offer at that time. One caution is to never promise any employee anything at the start, from a future increase in pay to a promotion. Your employees must understand that you will commit to the success of the company as a whole and that their assistance in the process will not be taken for granted; however, they must decide for themselves whether remaining with your company will most appropriately meet their needs and goals as time progresses.

Consider including interns as part of your staff. Never underestimate their value in terms of financial savings to your company and their motivation to complete tasks. Because interns are often seeking to gain experience either for college credit or to help boost their resume and hiring potential, they are often skilled in a particular area of expertise and highly motivated to do an outstanding job. Working with interns also allows you to observe their work performance before considering them as potential candidates for hire in the future.

Volunteers are another great resource. These individuals are usually looking to make a positive contribution to a company or cause that fits their interests and passions, time schedule, and/or preferred location. Although volunteers work for free, high school or college students may need community service hours in exchange for their service. Working with volunteers in the beginning stages of your business can help you to determine if any adjustments need to be made with regard to the tasks they undertake and to see if it is necessary to actually hire someone in that role. As your company develops and you begin to hire staff, be sure to adjust the duties of your volunteers so that they are not working as much in the latter stages of your business as they did during the start-up phase when you were unable to hire paid staff persons. Properly adjusting the duties of your volunteers will help to make a clear distinction between paid and volunteer staff.

2. Employee manuals

Develop policies pertaining to work days and hours/shifts, holiday schedules, lunch schedules, leave time (i.e., sick, personal, vacation, Family Medical Leave Act/FMLA), benefits and perks (i.e., medical insurance, performance bonuses, tuition reimbursement), Internet use, cell phone use, incident reports, and other aspects needed to help your business to operate efficiently and effectively. *Leave no stone unturned.* If you feel a situation will become a potential issue, be proactive and develop a policy in advance (i.e., confidentiality, non-compete clause, parking, tardiness).

Using other business' employee manuals as a guide can help to ensure that your company's policies are not in violation of government protections pertaining to employee rights and business operations. Also, know that your manual will need to be updated as your company continues to exist and expand and as laws change. Never allow your manual to become outdated; this may communicate a lack of concern for your business and/or your employees.

3. Include technology

There is a vast array of technological advances and on-line programs designed to help automate, evaluate, and/or update your processes for hiring, payroll, banking, tracking inventory, selling products, scheduling appointments, conducting meetings, responding to e-mails, monitoring facilities, organizing facility maintenance schedules, and more! Speak to other CEOs about the products and services they use to help ease their workload. Research a variety of companies that offer these products and services and compare offerings, quality, prices, reviews, and other information.

4. Evaluation procedures

All excellent CEOs have a plan for monitoring their success, that of their employees, their products, and their services. Evaluation is critical to the success of any company. Both formal and informal observations are necessary, and must be done on a frequent basis. Set clear expectations, communicate them to your staff, measure your expectations, and make adjustments to the processes, programs, and/or staff as is necessary. Remember to set your expectations based upon your company's mission and vision, which is *the heart of your company*. This will help you to remain focused and unbiased in your evaluations.

Furthermore, model what you expect from your staff (paid and unpaid), retailers, and service providers. This will encourage others to take you seriously and motivate them to carry out your expectations on a daily basis.

Q & A

List 3 systems/procedures that you need to implement so that your business operates more efficiently and effectively.

_____
_____
_____
_____
_____
_____
_____
_____
_____
_____
_____
_____
_____
_____
_____
_____
_____
_____
_____
_____

CHAPTER 9

SETTING YOUR PRIORITIES

Every entrepreneur enters into business understanding that he/she must work hard. However, many do not expect to keep working so hard—years into their entrepreneurship. If you have genuinely invested time, money, and training into your business on a full-time basis for over 5 to 7 years, and you are still working just as hard as you did in year 1, you may need to stop and evaluate your business practices. For instance, make sure you are not a workaholic or that you do not have a great need for control. Remember, one reason you started your business was so that you could take it easy and work on your own terms while making money!

1. Put God first

If you feel that God has given you your entrepreneurial vision, then be sure to give Him thanks and to glorify Him in all that you and your company do for the benefit of others. Model Godliness before your staff, clients/customers, and all with whom you have contact during the work day. Be sure to attend Church, Bible study, and other Church functions so that you can refresh your connection with God. Pray before going to work and pray throughout your work day. While you may experience a few bumps along the way, your faith will enable you to trust that God will guide you as CEO.

2. Attend to your needs

If you do not take care of yourself, you will have nothing to give to others. You will find that a lack of rest and poor diet may tend to dampen your mood and hinder your work performance. You may even be a little gruff with those around you. So, to avoid this, try incorporating the following suggestions.

- Eat a healthy balanced diet consisting of lots of fruits and vegetables.
- Drink 6 to 8 glasses of water.
- Exercise each day.
- Laugh with a friend.
- Enjoy your favorite hobbies (Your business is NOT a hobby!).
- Go to the spa.
- Take a vacation.
- Take a day off—especially if you are sick.
- Visit your doctors (primary care, optometrist, dentist, etc.) on an annual basis.
- Leave work at work—even if you are working from your home!
- Get 7 to 8 hours of sleep each night.

Taking care of yourself is one of the most rewarding things you can do. If you have no time for yourself and you are the CEO, then maybe you should appoint someone to take over for a while—if that is what it will take for you to attend to your own needs. You are your business. If you are suffering, then your business may suffer as well.

3. Spend time with your family and friends

Spending time with your family and friends will help you to remain true to yourself. Like many entrepreneurs, you decided to start your own business so that you could have more time to spend with your family and friends. You wanted flexibility in your schedule to be able to take your kids to school, pick them up from school, and to attend their practices, recitals, and games. Perhaps, you even began your business so that you could travel with your family and friends.

Do not take your loved ones for granted by allowing your business to consume your time. Include your family and friends in your business as well as spend time with them outside of your business. Your relationship with your family and friends can be a tremendous motivator during the difficult times of your business. Often times, your family and friends are your biggest supporters. If necessary, keep photos of your family and friends in your office so that you have a constant reminder of your number one fans!

4. Talk to your employees

Your employees will often be honest about work conditions—if you have a good professional relationship with them. So, focus on acknowledging their contributions to projects, their department, and the company in general. Encourage your supervisors and managers and even team members to recognize each other's efforts. In fact, encourage teamwork amongst your staff through staff luncheons, company outings, family fun days, etc. so that your work environment is a pleasant one for staff and others impacted by your company. Your company's reputation carries a lot of weight in the business world and your surrounding community.

Q & A

1. Describe the main reason for starting your own business.

_____
_____
_____
_____
_____
_____
_____
_____
_____

2. Take a moment to list your priorities.

_____
_____
_____
_____
_____
_____
_____
_____
_____
_____

CHAPTER 10

MAKING A BOLD MOVE

One issue that often surfaces (or lingers in the back of many minds) is when to leave your *day job* in order to start your own business. The only one who can ultimately address this issue is YOU! This issue requires a great deal of thought and prayer. When you make such a bold move as leaving your job, you must be absolutely sure it is the right decision for you and your family.

1. Retirement transition plan

If you will be retiring within the next 5 to 10 years, use that time to transition into your new business venture. Determine your calling and apply other tips in this book as applicable to your business. Invest a small portion of your salary to help start your business so that everything will be in place by the time you retire. Do not share your plans with your current supervisor or colleagues; however, if they happen to discover you are either starting or have started your business, share only what you are most comfortable sharing and keep the conversation brief—particularly while you *are on the clock*.

Once you actually retire, take time to enjoy your retirement. Since your pension will cover your living expenses, do not feel the need to begin your new business venture the day after you retire. Instead, take a vacation; spend time enjoying your family; sleep in late; or do whatever it is that will make YOU happy! Begin your new role as the CEO of your new company when you are ready—and not a moment sooner.

2. Exit strategy

If you are ready to leave your current job, then plan an exit strategy. Plan as if you are about to retire because essentially you are retiring from the world of work as you have known it for so many years. You will soon be venturing into your new business as CEO after you implement the exit plan that will work best for you. So, since you already have a job, utilize time outside of your work schedule to determine your calling and then implement various aspects of starting your business as outlined in this book, according to your business' needs. Invest as much of your current salary into your business as possible based upon the degree of your desire to leave your current job. For example, if you want to leave your job in 2 years, your investment will be less than that of someone who wants to leave his/her job in 1 year, 6 months, 3 months, or immediately. Also, set aside a portion of your salary to build an emergency fund in order to cover your household, personal, and/or family expenses for 3 to 12 months in case you are unable to immediately generate a steady income. These strategies should prevent you from spending your retirement, 401K, 403B, or any other savings you may have accumulated throughout your career—unless absolutely necessary.

When developing your exit strategy, you will need to be extremely focused so that you can *stay on track* with the timeline that you have given yourself to have everything in place. The amount of time you need depends mostly on you, your will, and your desire to see your vision become a reality. Therefore, be wise in all of your decisions so that you will not find yourself being tempted to reluctantly re-enter the workforce in order to supplement your savings or business in its start-up phase. When you develop the proper exit strategy, you will increase your opportunity to be able to smoothly transition into your new role as CEO of your own business, with little concern for finances.

3. *Quitting cold turkey*

Quitting a job without a plan is rough—especially if you do not have an emergency fund and you are trying to build your business from scratch! However, if you strongly feel that God is calling you to leave your current job in order to pursue your business on a full-time basis, then who can argue with that? When God has called you to do something, He will prepare you and supply all your needs along the way—just as He did for our forefathers in both the Old and New Testament.

One rule of thumb for being in the position to leave a job on short notice is to practice living within our means. This makes letting go of the security and familiarity of our *day job* a little easier. However, even in the midst of our indebtedness and stress, God asks that we let it all go, trust Him, and follow Him for the sake of the call. We are all called to serve in different capacities. If God has called you to do something, He will make a way for you to succeed. You only need to be obedient to the call and work diligently to make the vision a blessing for those whom God brings to your field of missionary service. Therefore, if you feel God is leading you to take that leap of faith by leaving your job to pursue His agenda, then determine your specific calling, pray, and apply the principles of this book as needed in order to develop your business. Also, be sure to leave your job on good terms and give at least 1 to 2 weeks' notice. You never know, your current employer may become one of your largest clients/customers after you start your own business, so *do things in decency and in order*.

4. Laid off or let go

Sometimes we do not have a choice as to when we leave our job due to either being laid off or let go. While an involuntary exit is never easy, it can be just as advantageous as a voluntary exit.

For those of you who have been wanting to start your own business, but never quite had the courage to leave your job, now you do not have to feel guilty about trading a steady paycheck for an uncertain and potentially sporadic stream of income. While you may not wish to invest much of your severance or unemployment benefits and/or insurance into your new business venture, you will need to consider investing a great deal of time into turning your vision into a reality. Evaluate your circumstance carefully and invest in your business wisely. Whether you have been laid off or let go, you will need to work as quickly as possible to begin your business so that you will soon be able to generate a steady stream of income.

The hardest decision for those who experience an involuntary exit will be whether to return to their previous job after the lay off period ends or to return to the workforce with another company. However, if you view your situation as a God-given opportunity to pursue your calling, then know that God will take care of you. So, pray and apply the principles of this book as needed in order to grow your business.

5. Consider your family

If you have a family, you must consider their needs. Granted, if God has called you, He will provide for your family in the process. However, you must include them in the agenda that God has given you as is appropriate. Even though everyone has a different calling, your family will ultimately be a part of your calling by virtue of being in the same household with you. If you are called to be a florist, you must help your family to adapt to what this means for the family as a whole, and the same is true for an author, pastry chef, or consultant. Your family will need to be aware of your new duties, schedule, and whatever else your new business venture and role as CEO entails. Your family's support is one of the keys to your success. So, draw them in through your passion and determination to succeed; do not discount the value of their support or take them for granted.

6. Lifestyle adjustment

Transitioning into your new business may require a bit of a lifestyle adjustment. You may need to consider downsizing and/or changing your spending habits in order to begin and operate your business. If adjustments are needed, find ways to compensate so that you and/or your family and friends do not feel like your business is taking away from your lifestyle and relationship with them. For instance, while you may not be able to go to a movie and dinner every weekend, you may want to consider hosting a bi-weekly or monthly pot-luck dinner and movie night at your home. Your family and friends will enjoy a fun and relaxing atmosphere. Instead of going to the spa, consider spending quality time with your daughter, sister, mother, grandmother, aunt, or friend painting each other's nails and doing each other's hair. Instead of going to the gym, consider inviting a group of friends to play basketball, softball, or ride bikes at your home, in your neighborhood, or at a local park.

If you need immediate cash to pay your bills and/or invest into your business, you might consider selling some of your items. Realize that you have probably made good use of most of the things in your closet, home, and/or garage, so parting with them for almost any amount could be helpful to your family and/or business needs. Even consider selling your car and using only 1 car or trading in your car for one that you may like, which is less expensive and/or has a lower interest rate. If your mortgage is extremely expensive, evaluate the space that you actually need. If you do not need as much space, then consider a smaller home, condo, townhome, or apartment.

Know that whatever lifestyle adjustments that may be necessary at the start of your business may only be temporary. As your business grows and your financial situation improves, you will find it rather easy to comfortably afford some of the things you once sacrificed. Perhaps, you might find that you no longer desire those things later in life. Who knows? If you need to make adjustments, then do so accordingly and with the appropriate spirit. This can help you to avoid family distress, foreclosure, repossession, and other legal situations in the future. So be proactive and wise.

Q & A

Step 1:
Be honest with yourself about your intended level of commitment towards making sure your business is successful. Nothing will happen until you take action.

Step 2:
Think about your situation and set 2 realistic goals for starting and maintaining your business so that it is successful—both in the immediate and distant future.

_____
_____
_____
_____
_____
_____
_____
_____
_____
_____
_____
_____

CHAPTER 11

PLANNING FOR YOUR BUSINESS' FUTURE

Planning for your business' future is as equally important as planning for its beginning. Every CEO needs to be sure he/she has a succession plan in place in the event of his/her disability, retirement, or death. Your business should not cease to exist simply because you are no longer present. Your business is your legacy and should exist for as long as possible so that others may continue to benefit from the unique services/products which your business provides.

With the input of all necessary parties, it should be relatively simple to ensure that all of the financial, legal, and other matters are properly addressed upon your absence from your business. So begin your succession plan right away while you are able to do so because there is so much more to consider than what is included in this section.

1. Your team's input

Speak to your legal advisor, insurance agent, and tax preparer to be sure that everything is in order. If you are working with a business partner, be sure to consider him/her in this process. In addition, be sure your Board of Directors is aware of your succession plan. Everyone will need to *be on the same page*.

2. Your family's input

Another important group to include in your succession plan is your family. Make them part of the entire process so that they will be clear about your intentions upon your absence. Also, make sure your family is at ease with your decisions so that they are able to properly handle questions and/or paperwork as needed—particularly if they have no interest in working at the company in your absence.

Q & A

1. What are your thoughts towards having a succession plan?

_____
_____
_____
_____
_____

2. When would you like to retire?

_____
_____
_____

3. What would you like to achieve as CEO prior to retiring?

_____
_____
_____
_____
_____
_____
_____

4. Who would you like to see serve as your successor? Why?

5. Who do you need to include in your business' succession planning? Why?

BONUS TIPS

1. Business certifications

Obtaining business certifications can be very advantageous to you and your ability to maintain a profitable business over time. Review the guidelines for becoming certified as a minority or female-owned business and any other local, national, and international certifications for which your business may qualify. These certifications will allow you to bid for corporate and government contracts which can be very lucrative. These entities are often mandated to solicit, accept, and even award contracts to businesses that meet certain criteria. So, review the guidelines and complete the paperwork if you qualify. If your business does not currently meet the criteria, then work towards being able to meet the criteria in the future.

2. Financials

Be sure to maintain accurate financial records. Seek the assistance of a reputable CPA/Tax Preparer who is certified to complete taxes for your particular type of for-profit or non-profit business. If you are unable to afford a bookkeeper or accountant, maintain your own books on a daily, weekly, and monthly basis. Properly recording your business income, expenses, and deductions will save you money and time in the long run.

Maintaining financial records that are both up-to-date and accurate are critical to the success of your business. Avoid fraud and excessive spending at all costs! Save your receipts, bank statements, invoices, and other financial records. Set aside time each day or week to review your finances—even if you have hired someone; as the CEO—you should always have an idea of how well your business is doing financially.

3. Give your business time to grow

Things do not always happen when we expect them to. So, give your business time to grow. If you focus on your business on a part-time basis, you may not see success at the same rate as someone who commits him/herself fully to his/her business. Also, just because you commit yourself to your business on a full-time basis, you may not necessarily experience an immediate rush of success—especially if you have not properly structured your business. Nevertheless, you must be persistent. You cannot give up on yourself or your business.

Set realistic goals for yourself and your business. Invest as much time, money, and training as is realistic for your situation based upon your finances, family, health, etc. Make sure that you incorporate all of the areas discussed in this book which are applicable to your business needs. Then, market your service and/or product through various sources—both free and paid. Marketing is the most important vehicle for any successful and profitable business. Although you may have a quality service or product, you cannot make a significant profit if only a few people know about it. Take nothing for granted. Give their business time to grow, but work your *marketing magic* to make things happen!

4. Keep it simple

Do not try to do everything or try to *save the world* through your business. There are people who need and are willing to pay for the unique assistance that only you can provide. If you find that you have several business ideas, instead of forming multiple businesses, determine the commonality among each of your ideas for business. Then, include them under one business umbrella. Think of it this way: a hair care company may sell shampoo, conditioner, styling gel, hair brushes, and flat irons—everything fits under hair care. Other companies may focus on resolving household concerns, so they have a number of household cleaning products, appliances, and décor—yet, everything fits under household goods. Another example is that of a department store. While the store may cater to a variety of customers such as moms, dads, teens, children, homeowners, blue collar and white collar workers, the store markets a number of products and/or services to include: clothing, food, a beauty salon, a portrait studio, auto repair, work wear, toys, kitchen appliances, and more—and, this is all found in one store! This business model works and it is simple enough to work for you, too. Your legal advisor and tax preparer can assist you in properly setting up your business and its finances—no matter how much your business expands.

Q & A

List a bonus business tip based on your own experiences that you feel should be included in this section.

_____
_____
_____
_____
_____
_____
_____
_____
_____
_____
_____
_____

BUSINESS RESOURCES

There are several associations and organizations to assist you in your business endeavor. Thanks to the Internet, you can find virtually everything you need for your specific business. Below is a list of resources that you can contact for assistance so that you can ***start a business and be your own boss***! This is only a partial listing, so please consult other CEOs and attend business networking meetings in order to learn about additional resources in your area.

- Small Business Administration
- Internal Revenue Service (IRS)
- Secretary of State Office
- Regional/Local Chambers of Commerce
- Business Guilds and Trades Associations
- Professional Organizations
- Public Library
- Local Bookstore

Q & A

List other business resources that you have learned about that you would like to share with other CEOs.

_____

_____
_____
_____
_____
_____
_____
_____
_____
_____
_____
_____
_____
_____
_____
_____
_____
_____

AFTERWARD

Now that you have finished reading this book, it is time for you to apply what you have learned. It is your turn to determine your calling in order to either start your business or evaluate your existing business and make adjustments wherever necessary so that your business can experience growth and success. Since you are the CEO of your own business, you will need to do what will work best for you and your business. Therefore, take care of the basics; invest in your company; find your ideal paying market; work with quality people; develop a CEO mindset; systematize your business; set your priorities; and make a bold move, Mr./Ms. CEO!

BUSINESS JOURNAL

Step 1:

Take time to reflect on your business and all that is discussed in this book. What are your thoughts about what you have learned?

_____
_____
_____
_____
_____
_____
_____
_____
_____
_____
_____
_____
_____
_____
_____
_____
_____

Step 2:

Develop a brief outline of your next steps.

3. Write a brief bio. Include what you feel is most important for your ideal clients/customers, lenders, and investors to know about you?

Dr. Carletta D. Washington

ABOUT THE AUTHOR

Carletta D. Washington, Ed.D.
Personal & Professional Development Specialist

I founded the Education 4 All movement as a resolution to the negativity that was directed toward the education system, students, parents, and educators. I believe that we can improve our future if we each do our part to help both ourselves and others.

Let me assure you that I am neither naïve, nor foolishly optimistic; I have had my share of negative experiences over the past 20 years. Fortunately, I did not wallow in my sorrows (for long) and my family, friends, and colleagues did not allow me to do so either!

As a result, I have been blessed to extend my commitment to helping others beyond the school setting. Thanks to many supporters over the years, Education 4 All, Inc. has evolved into a comprehensive program designed to assist teens and adults to be their best at home, school, work, and in the community!

Will you join me in supporting Education 4 All in the areas of college & career exploration, classroom management, stress reduction, and leadership development? I am confident that you and I can make a positive impact on the lives of teens and adults everywhere!

***

I have written this book so that you and other entrepreneurs may be able to avoid the pitfalls that I have experienced in the developmental stages of my business. My desire is for entrepreneurs to have a prosperous and sustainable business for decades to come!

MISSION

Helping teens and adults be their best at
home, work, and in the community

IDEAL AUDIENCE/CLIENTS

Teens and adults wanting to learn strategies to be their best

Education is a life-long process. Our customized individual and group training sessions provide evidence-based strategies which can easily be incorporated into your existing personal and professional environment.

4 places are impacted most by human behavior and interaction: home, school, work, and the community.

All teens and adults can be their best when they have the tools and strategies to do so.

EDUCATION 4 ALL PROGRAMS

Education 4 All is excited and ready to help students, teachers, parents, and the greater community in these core areas:

- College & Career Exploration
    - College Preparation & Scholarships
    - College/Scholarship Essay Assistance
    - Career Transition
- Stress Reduction
    - Early Teen Program (Ages 12-15)
    - Older Teen Program (Ages 16-20)
    - Adult Program
    - Parent Resources
        - Weekly Radio Program
        - Quarterly Parent Magazine
        - Missouri County Community Resource Guide

- Classroom Management

- Leadership Development

    o Employee Leadership Program

    o Executive Leadership Program

Program Benefits

1. Our programs are offered on an individual or group basis.

2. We offer half- and full-day sessions.

3. Materials are included with our programs.

4. Our programs are based on proven methods, which can easily be incorporated into your existing personal and professional environment.

For information about our programs and advertising opportunities, visit:

www.education-4allinc.com

****

If you would like Dr. Carletta D. Washington to speak to your school, Church, community, or business, contact her TODAY!

Carletta@education4allinc.com

Education 4 All, Inc.
P.O. Box 38722
St. Louis, MO 63138

www.ingramcontent.com/pod-product-compliance
Lightning Source LLC
Chambersburg PA
CBHW051717170526
45167CB00002B/691